Soccer Playbook

Table of Contents

Welcome to MEGA Sports Camp 3
Dear Head Soccer Coach 4
A Day at MEGA Sports Camp 6
A Closer Look at the Sports Sessions 7
At MEGA Sports Camp 8
Head Coach Checklist 10
MEGA Sports Camp Age-Level Characteristics and Tips 12
What to Do When Kids Act Up 14
Keeping Kids Safe 16
Five-Day Soccer Curriculum 17
Day 1 18
Day 2 25
Day 3 31
Day 4 37
Day 5 44

©2004 by Gospel Publishing House, Springfield, Missouri 65802-1894. All rights reserved. No part of this book may be reproduced, stored in a retrieval system, or transmitted in any form or by any means—electronic, mechanical, photocopy, recording, or otherwise—without prior written permission of the copyright owner, except brief quotations used in connection with reviews in magazines or newspapers.

ISBN 0-88243-142-0
33-0107
Printed in the United States of America

Welcome to MEGA Sports Camp!

As Head Coach, you are part of an exciting sports opportunity for kids. MEGA Sports Camp offers a unique combination of three important components:

Sports fun!
Offering quality sports instruction is a key ingredient to the success of MEGA Sports Camp. High-action, coach-led sessions get kids in first to sixth grade moving. And the safe, positive environment guarantees the kids will gain confidence and self-esteem right along with athletic skills.

Community outreach!
Kids love sports, so they'll want to invite their friends to join in the fun. By promoting MEGA Sports Camp in your community, you'll probably have lots of kids choose to attend your sports sessions.

Life-changing ministry!
Unlike a lot of other sports camps, MEGA Sports Camp offers more than just sports training. Kids also enjoy rallies with upbeat music, Bible stories, and ultracool object lessons that encourage character development for every kid.

This ***Soccer Playbook*** is filled with the drills and activities needed to lead effective Sports Sessions.

Dear Head Soccer Coach:

Thank you for being a part of MEGA Sports Camp! You have a wonderful opportunity this week to impact kids in athletic and spiritual ways.

You will demonstrate the skills and drills for the players this week. Prior to camp, read the **Soccer Playbook** and choose the drills you want to run. Keep in mind that your players will have varying levels of soccer knowledge and varying skill levels. Think about ways you can adjust the drills to meet the needs of your players. Some drills are more suitable for younger or older kids and are marked as such. Most drills, however, can be used with any age group. After explaining the drill to the entire group, have the older kids play on one side of the field while the younger kids play on the other side. For some drills, you will want all the kids to play together.

Be aware of how well your players are learning a skill and how much they are enjoying a drill. Adjust the drills to help the kids learn and to keep them from becoming frustrated. This experience should be fun!

Because some of these kids may know little about soccer, describe the rules of the game and common terms as you explain the drill. Incorporate the rules and the terms as you teach to keep the players interested and to help them learn along the way. Circulate among the groups as they are practicing to answer questions or to lend a hand.

Be positive! Encourage the kids in everything they do. Kids probably won't master these skills in one Sports Camp, but they will decide if they like the sport, if it's fun, and if they will play again. More than that, these kids will be influenced by your attitude. If you are upbeat and encouraging, your players will respond positively and will feel good about themselves, the sport, the church, and you. Urge your Assistant Coaches to encourage the players every chance they get. Enthusiasm is catching!

Your Assistant Coaches may or may not be familiar with soccer. These people love God and love kids. Like you, they are wonderful to donate their time and energy to this camp. Help the Assistant Coaches feel comfortable with the sport and the format of the Sports Sessions. Meet with them prior to camp to go over some basics of the game. This can be on a Saturday morning, on a weeknight after work, or whenever your schedule allows. Use the time to explain the camp game plan by telling them what skills will be covered and what drills the kids will learn. The Assistant Coaches may want to practice the skills and drills to help them understand. Be encouraging. The kids won't care if the Assistant Coaches are pros. Kids want to have fun. Help the Assistant Coaches feel confident. Camp should be fun for them too!

Think of a response device to keep the kids' attention. At the beginning of the week, tell them to listen for a key word, a whistle, or some other signal. Ask them to respond in a certain way when they hear it. Make this activity like a game. For instance, you could say, "When you hear me quack like a duck, you should immediately stop what you're doing and moo like a cow." Or, "When you hear me say 'Woof,' you should immediately stop what you're doing and sing 'And Bingo was his name-O.'" The kids will laugh and be alert to what you're saying.

Finally, pour yourself into your kids. Pray for them. Practice with them. Play with them. This will be a great week. Enjoy!

MEGA Sports Camp Team
Gospel Publishing House

A Day at MEGA Sports Camp

MEGA Sports Camp offers a mix of sports and other activities. Here's a sample schedule for one day.

Time	Event	Length	Location	Leader
	Opening Rally	15 Min.	Rally Zone	Rally Coach
	Sports Session 1	35 Min.	Sports Areas	Head Coach
	Coach Huddle 1	10 Min.	Sports Areas	Assistant Coaches
	Sports Session 2	35 Min.	Sports Areas	Head Coach
	Halftime Rally	10 Min.	Concession Stand	Concession Stand Coach
	Halftime Rally	15 Min.	Rally Zone	Rally Coach
	Sports Session 3	35 Min.	Sports Areas	Head Coach
	Closing Rally	15 Min.	Rally Zone	Rally Coach
	Coach Huddle 2	10 Min.	Rally Zone	Assistant Coaches

* On the last day, the Director may opt to invite parents to observe Sports Session 3 and the Closing Rally.

A Closer Look at the Sports Sessions

The first thing kids ask when they walk into MEGA Sports Camp is, "Are we going to get to play games?" That's why the Sports Sessions are intentionally designed to help the players practice. They'll improve their skills in the first two Sports Sessions, and in the third session they will get to play.

Sports Session 1: Skills Development
This session focuses on individual skill work and improving the players' abilities. Players may or may not compete with others.

Sports Session 2: Skills Development & Tactics
During this session, players review the skills they have learned or learn new skills. Then they practice the skills, using them in contexts that are more like competition.

Sports Session 3: Games
Most kids love game time. As Head Coach, you will set up games that are usually played in a smaller playing area. Assistant Coaches can help you organize the games and coach. This is low-level competition.

At MEGA Sports Camp

Your primary responsibility focuses on leading Sports Sessions 1, 2, and 3.

- Arrive early and prepare before the session begins.

- Set a goal of engaging the kids in a drill or activity within four minutes of arriving at each Sports Session.

- Follow the playbook, and try to complete two or three activities in every Sports Session.

- Synchronize your watch with other coaches. Stick to the schedule. It's helpful to assign this responsibility to an Assistant Coach.

More about the Assistant Coaches

You have other adults or teens available to help you. Their primary responsibility at MEGA Sports Camp is to build relationships with the kids and help the kids have a great time.

During the Sports Sessions, the Assistant Coaches help you set up the **Cones** and guide the kids as they practice. Let your Assistant Coaches know what to do.

During Coach Huddles, the Assistant Coaches meet with an assigned group of kids (a Huddle Group) and share stories from the *Coach Huddle Guide*. You are free during this time to prepare for the next session unless the Camp Director has asked you to lead a Huddle Group.

More about Coach Huddle Groups

At most MEGA Sports Camps, kids are assigned to a Huddle Group that is led by an Assistant Coach. These groups are NOT teams. You may regroup kids as needed for the Sports Sessions.

More about the Players

Kids register for and attend all the Sports Sessions in one sport of their choice. If you have a large group, you may want to divide them by age and ability.

Help the kids have fun. The Sports Sessions should make kids smile, laugh, and have a blast playing and learning together. Remember to coach from love and caring, not from a drive for perfection. Together the coaches and players should strive for an attitude of, "I'm going to work hard for you, and you're going to work hard for me, and we're going to have a blast together."

From the Field

We discovered that teaching the kids these simple signals improves sports time:

1. Any time the whistle blows twice, stop what you're doing and put the ball on the ground.

2. One whistle blast signals the beginning of an activity.

Head Coach Checklist

Before MEGA Sports Camp begins

❏ Read this playbook. The activities have been tested in many settings to make sure they work with kids.

❏ Examine the soccer facility. Keep the setting in mind as you plan the daily activities.

❏ Attend the MEGA Sports Camp training session. Meet the Assistant Coaches who will help at the soccer Sports Sessions. Allow them to look over the *Soccer Playbook* if they would like to become familiar with the activities.

❏ Check with the Camp Director for how to handle sports injuries. Record the plan on the safety page of this playbook (page 16).

❏ Gather sports equipment. You're reading one of the most important resources—the *Soccer Playbook*. Kids will be asked to bring a soccer ball and shin guards when they register, but you may want to have a few extras on hand, just in case. Here's a suggested list of additional supplies:

_____**Cones**

_____**Pinnies**

_____**Half Cones**

> **From the Field**
>
> Recommended for an average camp of 24 soccer players:
> - one soccer ball for each player
> - **Shin Guards** for every player
> - one **Whistle** for the head coach
> - a watch or clock to stay on schedule
> - 20 **Cones**
> - 20 **Half Cones**
> - 12 **Pinnies** (or enough for half of the kids) to designate teams during games

MEGA Sports Camp focuses on the individual, so here are some important points to remember during competition:

1. Do keep score when appropriate because in competition keeping score is part of the game.

2. Don't keep standings because the focus isn't on who wins.

3. Do control competition so it is fun and every kid has a good time. You may choose to control competition by allowing the Assistant Coach to play on the team that is behind. It helps to make the game more interesting.

4. Do care about the kids growing and becoming better athletes as well as developing character traits that make them valuable members of their teams.

5. Do interrupt game play for teaching moments as needed.

MEGA Sports Camp Age-Level Characteristics and Tips

Early Elementary: Grades 1 and 2

I am in a constant state of motion. Channel that energy into the drills and games.

I am still developing my eye-hand coordination. Keep activities simple and encourage me a lot.

I lack confidence and need adult approval. Be quick to give praise, but be sincere.

I enjoy repetition. Don't be afraid to do drills over and over. This is how I learn.

I have a short attention span. Keep instructions and talking short and to the point. Only talk one minute for every year that I've been alive if you want me to stay interested.

I want to be first, and I am still learning how to share.

I want to make friends. Help me understand and respect the rights of others.

Upper Elementary: Grades 3-6

I am full of energy and enjoy organized games. Provide clear and simple rules for me to follow.

I have developed good eye-hand coordination. I am ready for some of the more challenging drills.

I like to complain. Don't scold me for it. By listening to my complaints you help me feel valued.

I have frequent mood swings. Be patient. Bad moods will pass.

I am usually cooperative and agreeable. I usually know when I've done something wrong. Don't overreact. Accept my apology and move on.

I resent adults talking down to me, and I am sensitive to criticism. Treat me with the same kind of respect you expect from others. Be encouraging.

Friends are important to me. It is okay to let me and my friends be on the same team, but help me make new friends and accept others.

I have a strong sense of justice or fairness. Be careful not to show favoritism of any kind.

I am influenced by my teachers. Set a good example in attitude and actions.

What to Do When Kids Act Up

There are several basic reasons why a kid acts up.
- He wants attention.
- She is uncomfortable.
- He is afraid of failure.
- The tasks are too difficult or too easy.
- She is going through personal problems.
- He has an emotional or behavioral disorder.

Here are some things you can do when kids act up during the Sports Sessions.
- Remind the kid of the camp rules.
- Have the kid run a lap or do ten sit-ups.
- Have the kid sit out of a game or activity for a few minutes. (Limit this to a minute or two for younger kids and no more than five minutes for older kids.)
- Ask the kid to be your helper while demonstrating a game, drill, or activity.
- Say the kid's name as you give instructions.
- Have an Assistant Coach sit or stand next to the kid to give encouragement.
- Change to a new activity. Kids may be bored or overchallenged by the drill.
- Use praise and positive reinforcement to encourage kids to be respectful to others.
- Separate the kid from the rest of the group or send her to the Camp Director.

In extreme cases when a child is acting up continually, use a three-strike policy.

> Strike One: Make eye contact with the kid or say his name to get his attention. Tell him what behavior he needs to change.
>
> Strike Two: If the behavior continues, call the kid by name. Explain that this is his last warning.
>
> Strike Three: Have an Assistant Coach or other helper take the kid to the Camp Director.

Remember the point of this camp is to show Jesus' love to these kids. Kids at Sports Camp come from many different backgrounds and situations. Be sensitive to that. Do not respond to behavior with shock or anger. Correct behavior in a kind and loving manner. Do not be judgmental or condescending. You want Sports Camp to be a positive experience.

Be sure to share the rules of the camp with the campers. Remind them of these rules often. This way the kids know what is expected of them and will be less likely to act up. The Camp Director will provide the Sports Camp rules and the policy for discipline.

Notes:

Keeping Kids Safe

Include the safety and injury plans for your MEGA Sports Camp. These should be provided by the Camp Director.

Five-Day Soccer Curriculum

This curriculum was developed for a five-day soccer camp. Each day consists of three sessions approximately 30 minutes in length.

Day 1

For today's drills you will need **Pinnies, Cones,** and soccer balls.

Session 1: Technical Session, Dribbling

Warm-up Game—Tails

Do not form teams. Give each child a **Pinny** and have him tuck it into his shorts in the back to make a "tail" that is long enough to swing back and forth. Set boundaries in relationship to the size of your group. Explain the game:

1. Each player dribbles and tries to protect his tail while trying to pull out the tails of other players.
2. A player may not hold his tail to protect it. When a player pulls out a tail, he throws it to the ground. The player who has lost his tail must kneel where the tail landed until the game ends. He may steal tails from other players who come within reach of his kneeling spot. He may not leave his knees.

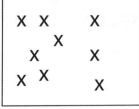

X = Players

3. The last person with a tail wins.

Variations: Play the game with designated tail colors. Allow the girls to play against the boys.

Introduction:

Emphasize three key points about dribbling:
1. They must change speeds.
2. They must change direction.
3. They must keep their heads up as they dribble. This is crucial to creative play.

Use any of the following drills during the technical session. They should be mixed in and around your instructional time on dribbling. Choose the ones that best fit your group and plan.

1. Elements on Command (good for all ages, use only as review for older players)

Stand in the middle of the grid. Tell the players to get their balls and begin dribbling around inside the grid. Have the players change speeds on your command. Instruct them to dribble three or four steps fast and then slow down and listen for the next command. After a few minutes of this pattern, have the players change direction on command. Mix elements.

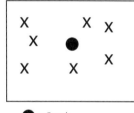

● = Coach
X = Campers with a ball

2. What's My Number? (good for all ages, only as review for older players)

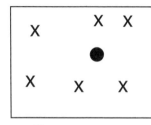

● = Coach
X = Players with a ball

Move freely in the grid while all the players dribble. Every few seconds hold your hand high in the air with one to five fingers raised. Have the players call out the number of fingers you have raised. This forces the players to keep their heads up while they dribble.

Variation: Let one of the players act as coach.

3. Beat the Crabs (good for all ages)

Evenly divide the players into two teams. Explain the game: The crabs (Xs) sit on the grass and move only by using their arms and legs in a sitting position. The dribblers (Os) try to move from one end of the grid to the other without going out of bounds. The crabs move on all fours to kick the balls dribbled by the Os out of bounds. Once the Os reach the end of the grid with their balls, they are safe, and the game resumes in the other direction. If a player loses her ball out of bounds, she becomes a crab (X). The last dribbler remaining wins.

Variation: Kids vs. counselors.

X = Crabs
○ = Players with a ball

4. Red Light, Green Light (good for ages 8 and under)

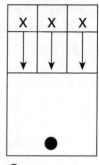

= Coach
X = Players with a ball

Explain the rules: When you yell "green light," the players are to dribble toward you. When you yell "red light," every player is to stop with her foot on her ball. If a player loses control of her ball, send her back to the starting line. The first player to cross the line where you are wins.

Stand at the far end of the grid. Put the players on the other end of the grid and start the game.

After someone wins, you may have the athletes play the game again, going in the other direction.

Variations: Add a yellow light and say "red" instead of "green" to trick players—they can only move on green.

5. Knock Out (good for all ages)

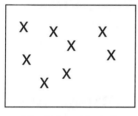

X = Players with a ball

Arrange a signal. Have all the players get in the grid and begin dribbling. When you give the signal, have the players try to protect their balls by dribbling away from others while trying to kick the other players' balls out of the grid. When a player loses his ball, have him sit and wait until the game ends. The last person in the grid with his ball wins.

Variations: Have girls play against girls and boys play against boys. You will have a girl winner and a boy winner.

6. Relay Races (good for all ages)

Have the teams line up relay-race style. Give the instructions for one of the following activities:

1. **Dribble down to a Cone, leave the ball, come back, and tag the next player in line. That player is to run down, get the ball, and dribble it back for the next player in line. Repeat the sequence.**
2. **Dribble through a set of Cones in a line. Weave through the Cones, and come**

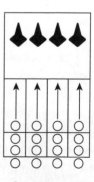

= Players
One ball per team

straight back beside the Cones. Then give the ball to the next player in line.
3. Dribble to a Cone 20 yards away using only the left foot. Turn around and dribble back using only the right foot.
4. Dribble down to me, pass the ball between my legs, regain the ball, and dribble back.

7. Body Part on the Ball (good for ages 8 and under)

Put every player in the grid. Each needs a ball. Tell the players what signal you will use to start the game. Explain that when you call out a body part (e.g., elbow, chin, knee, stomach), every player is to stop her ball and put that body part in contact with her ball. When you call out "dribble," the players are to resume dribbling until another body part is called.

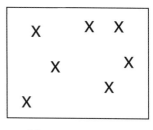

X = Players with a ball

Variation: Let a player call out a body part.

8. Follow the Leader (good for ages 8 and under)

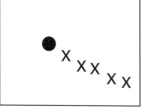

● = The coach or leader
X = Players with a ball

Have an Assistant Coach or older player begin dribbling the ball around the field anywhere he wants. Tell the players to follow and copy every move the leader makes.

9. Dribble through Cones (good for all ages)

Note: This drill is for instruction, not competition. Line up the players in two or more lines. Have them dribble through the **Cones** in a zig-zag pattern and form new lines

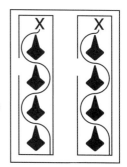

at the opposite ends from where they started. When all the players have dribbled and are in line, have them dribble back in the other direction.

Dribble pattern:
1. Right foot only
2. Left foot only
3. Both feet
4. Inside/outside of foot

10. Sharks and Minnows (good for all ages)

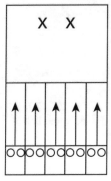

Line up the minnows (Os) along the end line with soccer balls. Have two players begin as sharks (Xs). Tell the minnows that when you give the signal to start the game they are to dribble through the sharks to the other end of the grid. Instruct the sharks to try to kick the minnows' balls out of play. Minnows who lose their balls become sharks. The last minnow dribbling wins.

Session 2: Tactical, one vs. one

1. Steal the Bacon (good for all ages)

Divide the players into two teams, and have them face each other. Number the players. Explain to the players that when you call out a number, the players with that number are to come out, try to gain possession of the ball, and dribble it behind their line. Roll the ball between the two lines and call a number (e.g., one). Keep score; the first team to steal five balls wins.

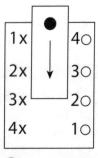

2. Look Mom, I'm a Goal
(good for all ages)

Divide the players into two groups of four. Tell two players to stand 15 to 20 yards apart and become goals by spreading their feet apart. Have the players in the center play against each other, trying to score by putting the ball between the legs of the player acting as goal. Play for one minute, then have the players and goals trade roles.

3. Take Me On! (good for all ages)

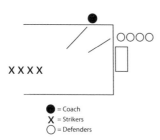

Divide the players into defenders and strikers. Tell the defender who is waiting at the goal to come out and take on the striker as soon as the striker touches the ball. Pass a ball to the striker. Don't have more than five players waiting in line at one time.

Variation: Have only three players in the defender line and everyone else in the striker line.

4. Race Me to the Middle (good for all ages)

Set up a small field with two goals. Line up the teams on opposite corners of the field. Collect all the balls. Tell the first player in line from each team to race down the sideline, around the corner, and through the goal. As the players are running, kick a ball to the middle of the field. The two are to sprint to the ball and play against each other, defending the goal they ran out of. End play when a goal is scored or the ball goes out of bounds. Repeat the process until all of the players have had a turn.

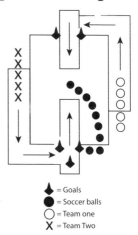

Session 3: Games

This session allows the players to practice what they have learned today in a gamelike situation. Divide the players into teams of four or five each. Divide the teams by age, but make exceptions for skill levels. Try to make the teams as even as possible.

Day 2

For today's drills you will need a watch, **Cones**, and soccer balls.

Session 1: Technical Session, Passing

Warm-up Game—Quick Draw

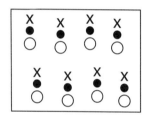

X = Player
○ = Player
● = Ball

Put the players in groups of two. Make sure the players are similar in size and age. Explain that when you call "quick draw," the players are to try to pull the ball back into their possession with the soles of their feet before their opponents do. Have the players jog in place the same distance from a stationary ball which is positioned between them. Call out "quick draw."

Variation: Make a game out of the drill. The first person to win three "quick draws" wins. The losers have to do a silly action or push-up because they lost.

Introduction:
Say: **The two most common types of passes in the game of soccer are the side-of-the-foot pass and the instep pass.**
Discuss the following key points about the side-of-the-foot pass:
1. This pass is used 80 percent of the time.
2. The foot is turned sideways and the ankle is locked.
3. The planting leg is bent slightly.
4. The ball is struck with the ankle side of the foot.
5. Face the direction of your kick.

Discuss the following key points about the instep pass:
1. This pass is used for longer passes.
2. The toe is pointed down and the shoelace part of the shoe strikes the ball.
3. Approach the ball from a slight angle.
4. The planting leg is slightly bent.
5. Finish the pass with the toe pointed down, not up.
6. Face the direction of your kick.

1. Yo-Yo Passing (review drill only for older players)

Put the players in two lines about 5 yards apart, each pair with a ball. Make sure each player has a partner and that each pair has a ball. Have the players use the sides of their feet to pass the ball back and forth. Walk up and down behind the lines watching and correcting.

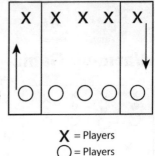

Variations: Right foot only; left foot only; one touch, two touch.

If you play one touch, explain that the meaning is literal. The players touch the ball only once. They do not dribble or trap the ball to control it. As a player receives a pass, he passes to someone else. If you play two touch, explain that this is also literal. The players touch the ball only twice: once to control it and once to pass it.

2. Passing for Points (use greater distance for older players)

Have the players pair up about 5 yards apart and make five side-of-the-foot passes at the goals formed by the other player's spread feet. The player with the best score out of five shots wins.

Variations: Right foot only, left foot only.

3. Passing Pressure Cooker (use greater distance for older players)

Line up the teams relay-race style, 7–10 yards from the small **Cone** goals. The goals should be 3 to 4 feet wide. Make sure each player has a ball. Time for one minute as the players try to pass the ball between the **Cones**. Every time the ball goes between the **Cones** without touching them, count one point. Have someone standing behind the **Cones** to pass the ball back and keep score. The team with the most points after one minute wins.
Variations: Right foot only, left foot only.

♦ = Cones
● = Coaches
X = Players with a ball

4. Storm the Castle (good for players 8 and under)

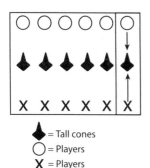

♦ = Tall cones
○ = Players
X = Players

Line up the teams facing each other with a set of tall **Cones** between them. Put the teams 5 to 7 yards from the **Cones**. Select a team to go first and make sure each member of that team has a ball. Tell the players that when you yell "ready, aim, fire," they are to try to storm the "castle" by knocking down the **Cones** with their balls. Conduct the activity. Set the Cones up and repeat with the other team. The team that knocks down the most **Cones** wins.

5. Beat the Clock (good for all ages)

Put the players in a circle around a random or organized set of **Cones**. Vary the size and number of **Cones** depending on the players' ages and abilities. Time the drill to see how long it takes for the players to knock down all the **Cones** using the side-of-the-foot pass and three balls. Repeat several times.
Variations: A larger circle, larger **Cones**.

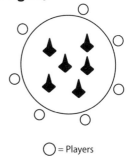

○ = Players
♦ = Cones

6. Never Ending Passing (good for all ages)

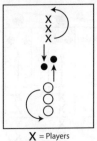

X = Players
O = Players
● = Balls

Begin the drill by having player X pass the ball to the first player O in the other line. Have player O duplicate the process. Continue in this manner until you are ready to stop the drill.
Variations: Right foot only; left foot only; one touch; two touch; see how long the team can go without making a mistake.

7. Take My Place (good for all ages)

Set up the players in a circle with a ball. Start the drill by having a player pass the ball to whomever she wishes. After she passes the ball, have her run and take the place of the person she passed to. Have the person who receives the pass continue this process as quickly as possible. Continue the drill until you are ready to stop play.

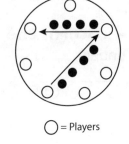

O = Players

Variations: Play with the one touch or two touch style.

8. Team vs. two (good for older ages)

O = Passers
X = Defenders

Have the players form a large circle with two players in the middle. Tell the outside players (Os) to try to make five consecutive passes without the inside players (Xs) touching the ball. If the Xs do not touch the ball they do five push-ups. If an inside player (X) touches the ball, rotate that player with the last O to touch the ball.
Variations: Add a second ball. Use one touch passes. Use right or left foot only.

Session 2: Tactical, Two vs. One to Goal

Introduction:
Say: **Yesterday, we worked on dribbling and taking people on one vs. one. Today we want to talk about working together and building our teamwork skills. The rest of the week, we will work on teamwork concepts with more and more players. Today we are talking about you and a teammate working together to score a goal against one defender.**

1. Wall Pass or Give and Go

Put the players in a passing line and make sure each has a ball. Stand in the receiving or "wall position." Have the players, one at a time, pass the ball to you and run to receive the ball back. Tell the players to form a line on the opposite side and repeat the drill going in the opposite direction. Repeat several times. Make sure the players pass with both feet.

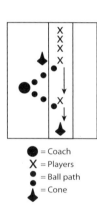

● = Coach
X = Players
• = Ball path
♦ = Cone

2. Beat the Coach

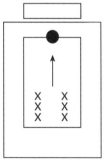

● = Coach
X = Players

Divide the players into two lines facing the goal. Stand in a defensive position, calling the players out two at a time. Tell the players to advance while passing the ball back and forth and trying to beat you. Passively defend the goal to let the players have success. Direct the players on what to do and when to pass—always encouraging. Emphasize support, movement, and teamwork.

Variations: Play more aggressively; put a player in to defend. Note: Keep the lines short.

3. Beat the Numbers

Modify the previous drill to emphasize defense. Encourage the defender (O) to "jockey" the two offensive players and wait for her

opportunity to steal the ball. Also encourage the
defender to be aggressive at the appropriate times.
Make sure a second goal is set up so the defender
can try to score on the two offensive players if a
steal is made. Use small goals for this drill.

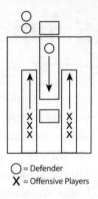

4. Lock on Target (good for younger players)

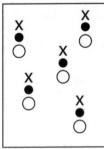

Put the players into pairs. Have each pair get one ball. Tell the players without balls to get inside the grid and begin moving around. Let them know they can go anywhere in the grid. Instruct the players with balls to enter the grid and follow their partners while dribbling. Let all the players know that when you yell "lock on target" they are to stop and those without balls are to form a goal with their legs. After the player with the ball takes his shot, have the players switch roles and continue the drill. Repeat the process until you are ready to end the drill.

Session 3: Games

This session allows the players to practice what they have learned today in a gamelike situation. Divide the players into teams of four or five each. Divide the teams by age with exceptions for skill levels. Try to make the teams as even as possible.

Day 3

For today's drills you will need **Cones**, soccer balls, and something flat than can be used for bases.

Session 1: Technical Session, Trapping or collecting the ball/Throw-ins

Warm-up Games—Freeze Tag or Soccer Baseball

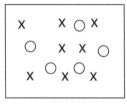

X = Players
O = Coaches

1. Freeze Tag

Place the players in a small grid adjusted to the size and age of the players. Get a ball for yourself and give each Assistant Coach a ball. Tell the Assistant Coaches and the players what the signal to start the game will be. Explain the game: When you give the signal, the coaches will begin dribbling inside the grid and trying to pass their balls off the players' legs. Players who get hit are frozen. Players who are frozen are to put their hands on their heads and yell for help. Unfrozen players may free frozen players by tagging them. Remind the other coaches not to pass too briskly. Begin the drill.

Variations: Players and coaches switch roles; boys vs. girls.

2. Soccer Baseball

Divide the players into teams, and lay out the bases as if you were preparing for a regular kickball game. Set up some soccer goals on the kickball field. Vary the length of the baselines and the size of the soccer goals according to the ages and skill levels of the players.

● = Coach/pitcher
X = Batting team
○ = Defensive
■ = Bases
⋀ = Goal

Explain the following rules:
1. The coach rolls the ball to the batter who kicks it as far as he can.
2. The kicker runs as many bases as he can before the defense kicks the ball into the goal. The runner is out when the ball enters the goal.
3. The kicker gets a point for every base reached before the ball enters the goal.
4. A foul ball (kick) is an out.
5. All players kick every inning. (There is no three-out rule.)
6. The defensive team must pass or kick the ball into the goal using only their feet to record an out.
7. Different defensive players must make outs in an inning.
8. The coach always pitches.
9. The coach can take a turn at kicking.

Session 1: Technical Session A
Trapping

Introduction:
Say: **Every player must learn to control the ball when it comes to her. You must learn to make the ball do what you want it to do and not let the ball dictate to you. Today we are going to work on trapping the ball with our feet, legs, and chest.**
Demonstrate trapping with the side of the foot and the sole of the foot. Set up a demonstration to look like the "Middle Man Drill."

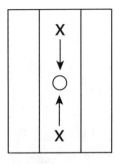

X = Players with a ball
O = Player in the middle

1. The Middle Man Drill

Separate the players into groups of three. Put one player in the middle and one on both sides of him about 5 yards away. Be sure the players on the sides each have a ball. Have the outside players facing the middle man begin the drill by passing the ball to the middle man. Tell the middle man to collect the ball, make a return pass, and spin around to repeat the process with the other player. Continue this process for one minute, and then have the players change positions. Repeat twice.

Pull everyone back in and demonstrate trapping with a leg. Emphasize taking the force out of the ball by dropping the leg away as the ball strikes the thigh. Send everyone back to their groups of three and have the outside players (Xs) toss a ball underhand to the middle man. Follow the same rotation as before. Pull everyone back in and do the same type demonstration for chest trapping. Emphasize leaning back to cushion the ball's impact on the chest.

Again, stress the importance of getting control of the ball with your feet as the ball drops to the ground. Send the players back to their groups to work on the chest trap.

Session 1: Technical Session B
Throw-ins

Introduction:
Demonstrate the proper throw-in technique: Over the head, two hands equally on the ball, facing the direction of the throw. Remind the players that the power comes from the thrower's back; his feet must stay in contact with the ground. Tell the players that there are two types of throw-ins: (1) standing and (2) step.

Discuss the standing throw-in points that follow:
1. Stand with both feet on the ground, shoulder-width apart.
2. Place hands equally on the ball.
3. Place the ball behind the head.
4. Face the direction of the throw.
5. Throw the ball. Remember the power of the throw comes from the back.
6. Keep feet in contact with the ground at all times throughout the throw.
7. Keep feet away from the line. If either foot touches the line, the ball goes to the other team.

Now discuss step throw-ins. Say: **The seven steps from standing throw-ins are the same except that the players take a step to throw the ball. The key here is that the back foot is dragged along the ground as the throw is being made.**

1. Show Me the Throw-in

Line the players up opposite a partner about 5 to 10 feet apart. Have them practice throw-ins by passing the ball back and forth. Make the receiving players use their different trapping techniques. Observe closely; give help and move on to the next pair.

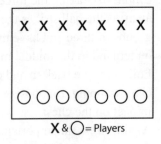

X & O = Players

2. Throw-in for Distance

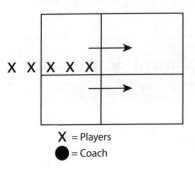

X = Players
● = Coach

Have each player stand behind a line and make three throw-ins for distance toward you. Use a **Cone** to mark each player's best throw. Find out who has the farthest throw-ins.

Variation: Hold a competition between groups.

Session 2: Technical Session, Three vs. One

Introduction:

Say: **This session is a continuation of the two vs. one passing instruction of yesterday. Today, we move to three vs. one.**

Note: This is a more difficult concept to learn. It can be frustrating to the players, especially the ones who didn't quite succeed at two vs. one.

Put the players in groups of three according to their skill levels. Closely control this session by being the defensive player. Emphasize positioning to the players so they can support the ball (i.e., the players shouldn't get caught standing behind a defender in line with the ball).

1. Monkey in the Middle

Group the players in fours. Make sure each group has one ball. Have three players in each group form a triangle around the "monkey" in the middle. Explain that the object is to pass the ball without letting the monkey touch it. If the monkey touches the ball the last person to make a pass becomes the monkey.

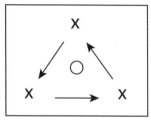

X = Players with a ball
O = Player in the middle

Variations: Make the triangle bigger or smaller depending on the skill level. Make the players play one or two touch.

2. Three vs. One, Take It to the Goal

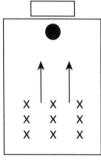

● = Coach
X = Players

Put the players in lines of three facing a goal approximately 20 to 30 yards away. You are the lone defender. Have the players start the ball with the middle player as the three attack the goal by using passing to try to beat you. Play aggressively enough to stretch the players' abilities, but let them succeed.

Variations: Make players use two touch or make set runs for the players to help them see how to run off the ball.

3. Beat the Numbers

Repeat the previous drill, but put the emphasis on defense. Encourage the defensive player to "jockey" the three attackers while waiting for an opportunity to steal the ball. Encourage the defender to be aggressive at the appropriate times. Place a goal for the defender so he can try to score on the three offensive players.

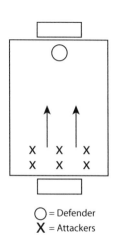

O = Defender
X = Attackers

4. Move to Space

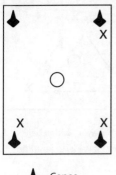

Start player X by the lower right **Cone** with the ball. He can pass the ball to either of the other two Xs. Both options are to the side. When the player passes the ball, the player who did not receive the pass runs to the open **Cone**. Continue this side pass–open **Cone** procedure as the defender tries to steal the ball. When the defender makes a steal, have him trade positions with the last X to touch the ball. **Note:** Make sure the ball keeps moving.

Session 3: Games

This session allows the players to practice what they have learned today in a gamelike situation. Divide the players into teams of four or five each. Divide the players by age first, with exceptions for skill. Try to make the teams as even as possible.

Day 4

For today's drills you will need **Cones** and soccer balls. If you choose to play soccer tennis, you will need access to a tennis court.

Session 1: Technical Session, Heading and Shooting

Warm-up Game—Pilots and Gunners or Soccer Tennis

1. Pilots and Gunners

Divide the players into two teams. Station the gunners on the sides of the grid. Make sure each gunner has a ball. Station the pilots at the end line. On your signal, have the pilots run between the gunners as the gunners kick the balls trying to hit the pilots below the waist. Make pilots who are hit gunners. The last pilot wins. Switch the pilots and gunners and have the athletes play again. Remind the players that injuring the pilots is not the object of the game.

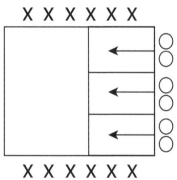

Variations: Pilots are coaches and players are gunners, or players are pilots and coaches are gunners.

2. Soccer Tennis: See Day 4, Session 2, Tactical Session.

This drill can be done from three different positions: A (guard to guard), B (guard to wing), or C (wing to corner). You will have time to choose only one. Instruct the defensive players to react to passes moving back and forth from offensive players. After at least two passes, instruct the defense to stop shots, passes, or penetration to the basket. Have the offensive team attempt to score. Bring new players on when the defense gains possession of the ball or the offense scores. You can make a game out of this drill if you want.

Session 1: Technical Session A, Heading

Introduction:
Touch on the proper technique of heading and run one short game, then move on to shooting. In heading you want to emphasize:
1. The ball should strike the forehead at the hairline.
2. The eyes should be kept open while the forehead is in contact with the ball.
3. The mouth should be kept shut.
4. The neck should be stiff and the chin tucked.
5. The power in this technique comes from the back.

For the younger children, start your teaching in a very basic manner by holding the ball and touching it to their heads in the proper position. Then, hold the ball and let them head against the ball while it is in your hands. Challenge older players a little more with pressure and competition while heading.

1. Toss to My Head (good for all ages)

Divide the players into groups of two. Have the players take turns tossing the balls underhand to their partners who head the balls back. Rotate the players every five tosses. Repeat the drill a few times. Walk behind the lines, giving instruction and encouragement.

Variation: Divide into groups of three. Have one player toss and the second player head the ball to the third player.

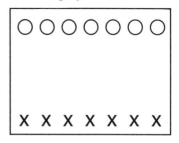

O = Players with the balls
X = Players

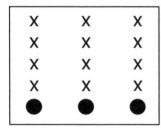

● = A coach with a ball
X = Players

2. Throw-Head-DUCK (good for all ages)

Line up the teams relay style. Toss a ball to the first player in line and have her head it back and duck. Repeat the process with the next player in line. After every player has headed the ball to you, have everyone stand. Have the last player run to the front of the line. Repeat the game.

3. Do the Opposite (good for all ages)

Line up the players shoulder to shoulder facing you. Get a ball. Tell the players to do the opposite of what you say. Start at one end of the line and say "head" or "catch" as you toss the ball to a player. Make players who fail to do the opposite of what you say sit down. Keep moving down the line. Practice a lot before you actually start eliminating players to find the winner.

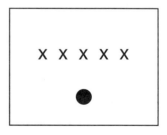

● = A coach with a ball
X = Players

4. Look, Mom, I'm a Bird (good for older players only)

Show older players the correct techniques for landing and catching themselves as they dive for the ball. Then, allow older players to attempt a diving header at the goal. Call out one player at a time, and toss the ball gently in front of the onrushing player.

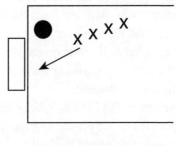

● = A coach with a ball
X = Players

Session 1: Technical Session B, Shooting

Introduction:
In shooting, emphasize the following:
1. Take a slight angle approach to the ball.
2. Make contact with the ball on the shoelace part of the foot.
3. Make sure your toes are pointed down and at the goal when finished.
4. Place the nonkicking foot beside the ball.
5. Lean your body forward at contact.
6. Land on your kicking foot after the shot is made.
7. Shoot for the far post instead of the near post when approaching the goal from an angle.

1. Shoot the Lights Out (good for all ages)

Make sure the teams are divided into four. Keep the teams small for more shots. Have two of the teams

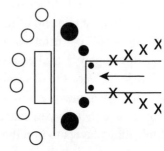

● = Coaches
X = Players shooting
○ = Players retrieving

shooting and two of the teams retrieving soccer balls. You and an assistant alternately roll out balls one at a time for a shot on goal. Have the players switch lines and repeat. After a couple rounds, have the shooters and retrievers switch. Be sure to get in lots of repetitions.

Variations: Right foot, left foot, bouncing ball, one touch, or two touch

2. Who Does Push-ups? (good for all ages)

Put the players in shooting lines as above. Place a counselor or coach in goal. Roll out a ball and let the player try to score on the counselor. Give the players ten shots. If the counselor stops all ten, the players do ten push-ups. If the players make one out of ten, the counselor does ten push-ups.

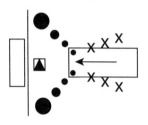

● = The coach with several balls
▲ = A counselor or coach in goal
X = Shooters

Variations: Make the players shoot from farther away, make the counselor not use his hands, put two counselors in goal with no use of hands.

Session 2: Tactical Session, Four vs. Two & Three vs. Two

Warm-up Game—Soccer Tennis

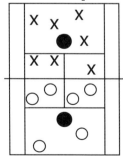

● = Coach
X = Players
○ = Players

Place a team on each side of a tennis court. If you are running this drill with younger players, have the Assistant Coaches play and serve. Having the Assistant Coaches play is optional with older groups. Let the players know they can't touch the ball with their arms or hands. Serve the ball over the net high and easy to land on the other side of the net. The other team must get it back over the net before it rolls. More than one player may kick the ball as long as it goes over the net. Award a point on every serve. A team earns a point whenever the opposing side fails to get the ball back across the net. End play when a team scores 15 points. If no tennis court is available, substitute a different game.

Variations: The ball must go over with a header; the ball must be touched by three different players; or, for the older players, the ball may not bounce more than three times.

Introduction:
Now that the players are up to three vs. two, emphasize on offense the importance of finding the open player and on defense the importance of how to support each other. On offense show the players how to position themselves to get a pass. On defense show the players how to send one player after the ball and have the other player hang back to support and to anticipate when to make an effort to steal the ball.

1. Two Against the World (good for all ages)

Set up four lines of players to attack the goal and two sets of defenders at the goal line. Put the ball in play and have the two defenders come out from the goal line and play against the four players on offense. Help the players see how to split the defenders and pass into open space.

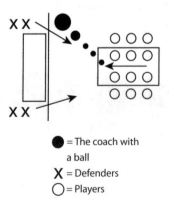

● = The coach with a ball
X = Defenders
O = Players

Variations: Younger players use three touch; older players use two touch; or defenders cannot come out until one pass has been made.

2. Three vs. Two (good for all ages)

Set the drill up the same as above. Limit the offense by having only three offensive lines. Continue to work on defensive positioning. Have the offense work at finding the open player. Stress that two cannot defend three; someone is always open.

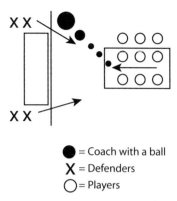

● = Coach with a ball
X = Defenders
○ = Players

Session 3: Games

This session allows the players to practice what they have learned today in a gamelike situation. Divide the players into teams of four or five each. Divide the players by age but make some exceptions for skill. Try to make the teams as even as possible.

Day 5

For today's drills you will need **Cones** and soccer balls.

Session 1: Technical Session, Heading and Shooting

Warm-up Game—Chickens and Wolves, Soccer Marbles, or Soccer Golf

1. Chickens and Wolves (good for all ages)

Divide the players into two teams: chickens and wolves. Have each chicken get a ball and get inside the grid. Keep the wolves outside the grid. Tell them that when you howl, they are to race inside the grid and steal the "eggs" of the chickens and kick them out of the grid. If a chicken loses her ball, she may try to regain it until it goes out of bounds. Once that happens she becomes a wolf. The last chicken left with a ball wins.

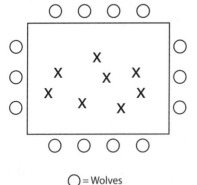

○ = Wolves
X = Chickens

Variations: The coaches are the wolves or send in the wolves one at a time.

2. Soccer Marbles (good for all ages)

Have each player get a ball. Divide the players into pairs. Explain the game: The first player kicks the ball out about 5 to 10 yards. When the ball stops the second player tries to hit the ball with a pass. If he is successful, he gets a point. When the second player's ball stops, the first player gets to try to hit it with a pass. The first player to hit five wins. Repeat the game, but have the players reverse roles.

2. Soccer Golf (good for all ages)

Divide the players into groups of four. Have all the players get balls. Allow the players to pick out a target (e.g., a garbage can, tree, fence post) and kick their balls toward the target. The player who takes the least amount of kicks to hit the target wins.

Session 1: Technical Session, Goalkeeping

Introduction:
Say: **Every player may have to play goalie at some time, so every player should have some knowledge of the basic skill needed to play goalie.**
Emphasize these points about catching the ball:
 1. Catch low ball with hands turned down.
 2. Catch high balls with hands turned up.
 3. Make sure the fingers form a "W" when catching high balls.
 4. Keep feet together when picking up the ball.
For the olders players review the above and talk about positioning and cutting down the angle of the shooter.

1. Catch and Show (good for all ages)

Put the players in groups of two and line them up opposite each other. Let them take turns throwing the ball to their partner at different heights and on the ground. This allows the players to begin to use the goalie skills taught during the introduction.

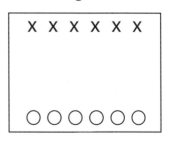

X = Players
O = Players

2. Hot Seat (good for all ages)

Position the goalie between two **Cones**. Form shooting lines on both sides of the goal. Have the lines alternate shots. After ten shots, replace the goalie.

If there is time remaining in the technical session, use it to review the things you have taught during the week in other technical sessions.

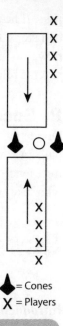

♦ = Cones
X = Players

Session 2: Technical Session, Four vs. Four or Five vs. Five

Introduction:
The key to any successful practice and game preparation is small-sided games. The 11 vs. 11 version of the game is made up of many small-sided games. As the lead coach in this session, have the teams play small-sided games in limited size areas. The game can be set up as defense vs. offense, regulation goals with even teams, small goals, more than two goals, no goals (keep away), or coaches playing. Put a series of restrictions on the games to make the players think and react.

Restrictions:
Place the following restrictions at your own discretion:
1. Play two or three touch.
2. The ball must be played to the coach to get a point.
3. One team gets three touches, the other unlimited.
4. Play keep away—five or more passes in a row by one team without the other touching the ball gets a point. The first team to score 5 points wins.

5. A wall pass or give-and-go is worth three points.
6. A player must beat another player on the dribble in order to pass.
7. Use four goals—each team defends two and scores on two.
8. One team gets a small goal, the other a regulation goal.
9. Restrict some players to certain areas of the grid and let others roam.
10. The coach gives extra points for good running off the ball.

Session 3: Games

During this session the past four days we have been playing games. You can again use this time for games. One of the things that has been popular during this final session on the last day is to have a game. (Coaches, counselors, and helpers vs. all the kids at one time is a popular event.)

Use good judgment on the size and ability differences of the kids, as well as the maturity level of the counselors and helpers.